Stock Market Investing

FOR BEGINNERS

Mordechai Goldstein

© Copyright 2018 - All rights reserved.

In no way is it legal to reproduce, duplicate, or transmit any part of this document by either electronic means or in printed format. Recording of this publication is strictly prohibited, and any storage of this document is not allowed without written permission from the publisher.

This publication is geared towards providing exact and reliable information in regard to the topics and issues covered. The publication is not a substitute for legal, tax, financial or professional advice. If such advice is necessary, a practiced individual in the profession should be consulted.

The publisher makes no guarantees regarding income as a result of applying the information contained in this document, and any liability regarding inattention or otherwise, by any usage or abuse of any policies, processes, or directions contained within is the solitary and utter responsibility of the recipient reader, and as such, for all intents and purposes, this document is to be considered as being "for entertainment purposes only." The reader should always seek the advice of a professional when making any legal, tax, financial, or business decisions.

Under no circumstances will any legal responsibility or blame be held against the publisher for any reparation, damages, or monetary loss due to the information herein, either directly or indirectly.

Any trademarks or brands mentioned in this publication are without any consent, permission, or backing of the trademark owner.

All trademarks and brands within this book are used only for the purposes of clarification, and are owned by the owners themselves, and not affiliated with this publication.

All copyrights not held by the publisher, are owned by the respective authors.

Table of Contents

Introduction	7
Chapter 1: An Understanding of Stocks	10
Company Ownership	11
Debt versus Equity	12
Stocks and Risk	13
Types Of Stock	14
Chapter 2: The Must-Know Stock Market Terms	16
Chapter 3: How The Stock Market Works	22
Stock Price Fluctuation - Causes	24
How Stocks Trade	25
Chapter 4: Stock Table or Quote – Interpretation	28
Conclusion	30

Introduction

The stock market; we all see financial analysis in the news, hear how companies' stocks are performing on the different stock exchanges and how upcoming companies are about to issue an IPO. The world's richest billionaires bet on stocks (Warren Buffett and his one million dollar wager is a good example). You then wonder, if the richest invest in stocks, then isn't that reason enough for anyone wishing to become rich to start thinking about investing in stocks too?

Well, if you've thought about investing in stocks, you know that the whole affair can seem pretty complicated for a complete beginner. You may feel at a loss as to why stock prices move up and down, why a company's release of financial statements affects its share price, why companies issue shares in the first place, and all the complex terminology that any ordinary person with no knowledge of the market just can't seem to wrap their head around.

Nonetheless, you know that now is the time to start investing in stocks. However, if you want to invest in stocks you first of all need to learn the basics. After all, you've got to learn to crawl before you can walk.

So you're pretty lucky that you purchased this book, because it will serve as that magic key to unlock everything you need to know about the stock market before you ever take any money out of your pocket and buy 30,000 shares of some company. This little book is the perfect solution for you, the beginner, as it will teach you all about these odd things, we have names for but can't really see, called stocks. You will learn what stocks are, the best time to buy them and the best time to sell them, as well as get some good tips on exactly what you need to do in order to become a successful stock market investor.

It has been proven time and time again that one can easily grow their wealth, through owning stock over a prolonged period. In fact, each Forbes 400 list member (which is basically a list of the top 400 wealthiest Americans) owns a large number of shares in private and/or public corporations in industries spanning oil, financial management, manufacturing, and cosmetics, among others. Although that's all besides the point. Quite simply put though, stocks are a worthwhile investment, and most investment portfolios contain stock.

Therefore, if stock is proven to grow wealth over time, and if all the richest Americans own stock, and if simply put it's a known worthwhile investment that makes up most investment portfolios, then obviously if you care at all about growing your wealth, then you need to get into the stock market!

Every year, more and more people get into the stock market. Though many years ago, the stock market was something that only the most wealthy had access to. Thus, it's quite wonderful that you actually have the option to get into the stock market and can grow your wealth the very same way the most wealthy do. Furthermore, due to an increase of wealth moving into the stock market, as well as numerous advancements in the trading technology, it's now easier than ever to jump into the stock market and start investing. However, there is one thing, and that thing is that very few people actually understand the stock market in all its glory and complexity, and to make matters worse, there is a lot of misinformation floating around about stock. Some people even consider the stock market to be some kind of get-rich-quick scheme. However, this is not true, because if it was a get-rich-quick scheme you wouldn't see the rich investing in it.

Anyway, the point is that before you ever put a single dime into the stock market. You've got to understand what exactly is going on there. And that is exactly what this book is going to teach you.

Chapter 1: An Understanding of Stocks

Stocks are a type of equity investment that reflects the percentage of a company that you own which is measured in shares. When you own shares of a company, you own a part of the company, and you therefore have the right to claim part of the company's assets and earnings. The more stocks you own in a company, the greater your ownership stake in the said company becomes. Corporations usually issue shares for purchase when they need to raise money, and this is accomplished through an IPO (Initial Public Offering).

During an IPO, companies price shares according to their market value and the number of shares being sold. Although the shares you buy from a company are traded on an exchange (like the New York Stock Exchange), the company utilizes the money received to grow its business. You, as the investor or trader, can buy and sell the company's stock continually on an exchange or keep it all for yourself; the company receives nothing because they only get funds from the IPO.

A long time ago, if you bought shares of a company, you were given a paper stock certificate as a way to verify your ownership of those shares. Unlike the past, your brokerage firm records the shares you buy in an electronic database. Due to the tricky nature of stock market investing you should take all of your investments seriously and treat them each as a business.

Mastering stock market investment basics should be your priority before buying your first shares. Although this won't make you a seasoned investor overnight, it will set you on the right path to becoming one. Knowledge is power, and with the right skills you'll soon be able to invest in the stock market with confidence.

Company Ownership

When you buy shares in a company, you become a shareholder, meaning you are one of the company's many owners, and to a certain extent you can claim everything owned by the company. Technically, this means that you own a certain percentage of the company's trademark, furniture, profits, contracts, etc, depending on the number of shares you own.

As a public company's shareholder, you get one vote for every share you buy. This means that you do not get to engage in the company's daily decision-making process regarding how the business is run. However, you can use your votes during the company's annual meetings to elect members of the board of directors. For instance, if you own shares of Google, you cannot dictate to the CEO how you think the firm should be run, though it is the role of the company's management to increase the value of your shares as well as that of the other shareholder's shares.

Theoretically, you, the shareholder, have the voting right to remove the management if they are not able to raise the value of your stock. However, this cannot happen in reality, because the stock owned by shareholders is not enough to give them the power to influence any major decisions within the firm; it is the entrepreneurs worth billions and large institutional investors that have this power.

As an ordinary shareholder, it is not a big deal if you cannot influence major decisions in a company in which you own shares. What is important is that your money is working for you, in addition to having rights to part of the firm's assets and profits. You definitely can be paid your share of the profits as dividends. The amount of profits you receive is directly related to the number of shares you own in the company: the more shares you own, the more the profits and vice versa. You can only claim your rights to the company's property in the case that it goes bankrupt. The way it usually works is that all the creditors get paid first, after which you get paid what remains.

You should note that stock ownership is as important as your claim on the firm's earnings and assets; the two go hand in hand. Moreover, your liability is limited, which means that if the company is in debt you are not liable. However, this is not the case with partnerships, where shareholders or partners are responsible for the company's debts.

Irrespective of what might happen, the only thing you can lose in the stock market is your investment, which are your shares. Your personal assets remain yours.

Debt versus Equity

You might be wondering why a company would sell its stock to hundreds or thousands of people when the founders could keep all the earnings for themselves. Well, companies usually need to raise some money at one point or another. They can achieve this through debt financing that entails borrowing money through bond issuance or from a bank, and equity financing that entails stock issuance.

Unlike debt financing, equity financing has more pros for the company. For instance, the company neither pays back the funds raised nor offers interest to the buyers. The shareholders, who are the stock buyers, only have to hope that one day their shares would be worth more than their buying price. Private companies usually issue their first sale of shares through an initial public offering, an IPO.

It is essential for you as a beginner to understand the differences between the equity and debt financing of companies. When you invest in debt through purchasing bonds, you can be sure that you will get back your money and the interest earned over the duration of the investment. On the other hand, with an equity investment, you become one of the business owners, a shareholder; hence, you bear all the benefits, losses, and risks of the company.

When you become a shareholder in a company, you are similar to being a small business owner who is not guaranteed any returns on their investments. Unlike the company's creditors, you, the shareholder, has less of a claim on the firm's assets. In the case the company liquidates or declares bankruptcy, the most absolute priorities first comes into play before you. This means that you are only paid after all the bondholders and banks, who are the firm's creditors, are paid their dues.

Despite the fact that the shareholders lose all of their investments if the company is not successful, you can earn a lot of money from your equity investment if the company is successful.

Stocks and Risk

When it comes to stock market investing, you should know that there are no guarantees. Although some companies can pay you dividends, several others will not. Furthermore, even though some firms have a history of paying their shareholder's dividends, they have no obligation to continue doing the same in the future. With no dividends, you can only make money from your shares if their value appreciates over time. However, if the company goes bankrupt, your investment becomes valueless.

On the flip side, if you put your money in investments with high risks, you stand the chance of getting higher returns on your investment. This explains why stocks have always performed better than bonds and saving accounts. Historically, investments in stocks have had up to 10% to 12% returns over a long duration.

Types Of Stock

Most people just assume that all stocks are the same. You will be surprised to learn that there are different types of stock. There are two major types of stock, common stock and preferred stock, with the former giving shareholders voting rights without any dividend payment guarantees and the latter offering shareholders no voting rights with a dividend payment guarantee.

Common Stock

This is the most common type of stock in the investment market. In fact, when you hear people talking of stock, this is what they are normally referring to because most stocks are sold in this form. The common stock shares reflect your ownership of a company and dividend claims come in the form of profits. For every single vote per stock you get as an investor, you get the right to elect the board members who ensure that the company's management makes the right decisions all the time.

Unlike many other investments, you can earn higher returns on your capital growth by investing in common stock over prolonged periods. The cost of you getting higher returns lies in the high risk associated with common stock investments. As mentioned before, you are also not paid until all the creditors receive their dues in the case of a bankruptcy.

Preferred Stock

Although preferred and common stock reflect your ownership of a company to some degree, the former does not come with voting rights, depending on the firm in question. When you invest in preferred stock shares, you are guaranteed dividends depending on the kind of preferred stock. This is unlike the common stock with no guaranteed variable dividends. Moreover, if you own preferred shares in a company, you are paid before the common stock shareholders are paid, but of course after the creditors receive their dues in the case of a bankruptcy.

However, in the case the company needs to raise a premium, they would buy your preferred shares because they are callable. According to certain people, preferred stock is more of a debt than an equity. You can consider preferred stock to exist between common stock and bonds.

Distinct Stock Classes

Although stocks are mainly categorized as common or preferred, companies can tailor the distinct stock classes as they want. A company can do this if they want only a specific group to own voting rights. Therefore, each of the distinct stock classes is given a unique voting right. For instance, a specific class of stock entailing the majority of shareholders could be given a single voting right per share, whereas another class of a select shareholder group could be given 10 voting rights per share.

The distinct stock classes are usually grouped into classes ranging from Class A to Z, depending on the number of classes. The BRK ticker, Berkshire Hathaway has a couple of stock classes only. In order to create a distinct form, its class letter is placed after the ticker symbol, like "BRK.A, BRK.B" or "BRKa, BRKb".

Chapter 2: The Must-Know Stock Market Terms

If you are to be successful at stock market investing, it is important that you know some stock market terms that you are likely to come across.

Stock Split

In most cases, publicly traded companies have a particular number of outstanding shares on the stock market. A stock split is a decision by the board of directors to increase the number of shares outstanding by issuing shares to current shareholders. For instance, in a 2 for 1 stock split, each shareholder who has one share is given an additional share. Therefore, if you had 10,000 shares, you end up having 20,000 shares. In a stock split, the price of the share is also affected. After the split in the above case, the stock price will be halved. Therefore, even though the number of outstanding shares has increased, and the stock price has changed, market capitalization remains constant.

Companies usually do a stock split when they see their share price increase too high or beyond the price levels of similar firms in the sector. Basically, the goal is to make the shares look more affordable to small investors even if the underlying company value has not changed.

Dividends

When you buy shares to become one of the company's shareholders, the company can pay you a part of their profits, known as dividends. However, the company's directors might decide not to pay out dividends, but rather use the money earned for growth and expansion.

If you want to get a good income, you can invest in a company that is known to pay their shareholders high dividends even if the share price does not increase as much in value. You can then use your dividends to buy more shares for even higher returns if the value of the shares goes up.

According to the Barclays Equity Gilt Study, which was carried out to find out the results of investing long-term, if you invest over a period of ten years, your average return on investment annually from inflation-adjusted stock is 5%. If you reinvest your dividends, you get the benefit of compounding interest.

The study utilized data that dates back to the 19th century to show the significance of reinvesting your dividend income. If 100 pounds were invested in equities in the late 1800s, it would be 191 pounds now if no reinvestments were made. However, if the dividends were reinvested, the amount would accrue to 28,386 pounds.

Ask or Offer

This refers to the lowest price that someone is willing to sell the security for.

Bear Market

This is a kind of market where the stock prices keep falling.

Beta

This is simply a measurement that shows the relationship between the stock price and the movement of the market.

Bid

This is the highest price at which a buyer is willing to pay for a security.

Bull Market

This is a market where stock prices keep rising.

Ex-Dividend

If you purchase ex-dividend shares, you are not entitled to the upcoming dividend that has already been declared.

On-Stop Order

This is a term that is used to refer to the intention of trading at a later time when the stock price reaches a particular top price.

Penny Stocks

These are low-priced stocks that sell at less than $1.00 a share

Bonus Issue

This is when a company issues you dividends in the form of shares instead of cash.

Rights Issue

This is when current shareholders can purchase shares at a special price based on their holdings of old shares. The share price in a right issue is usually lower than the market price.

Blue-Chip Stocks

Although blue-chip stocks have a reputation for being stodgy, boring and even outdated, they have worked wonders for the lives of non-profit foundations, retirees, and even conservative people because they can generate so much money over a long period of time. The phrase 'blue-chip' comes from the game poker where the most valuable chips are the color blue. The kind of companies that offer blue-chip stocks are usually top companies in America with a rich history.

Blue-chips are all about making profits; hence, their prosaic nature is not deserved. If you invest in blue-chip stocks, you can hold them for many decades, and it usually means that your family has access to a lifetime stream of income through dividends.

A relatively subjective criterion is used to categorize a company's shares as blue-chip. According to many professionals, blue-chip stocks have various attributes that are similar, including:

- High commercial paper and bond market credit ratings.
- Strong balance sheets with an average burden of debt.
- A competitive market place advantage due to franchise value, cost efficiency, or even control of distribution.
- A record of many decades of established stable earning potential.
- A large size of market capitalization and revenue in relation to businesses in America.
- Diversified geographic location as in the case of Coca-Cola, and varied product lines as in the case of General Electric.
- Long dividend payment records to holders of common stock that are uninterrupted.
- The dividends you receive increase in value payable to each shareholder.

The Industrial Average of Dow Jones

The majority of blue-chip companies make use of the industrial average, Dow Jones, to ensure that their positions in the industry remain the same. With great credit ratings and average levels of debt these companies can borrow money at a lower cost than their counterparts (their competitors) in the marketplace. Customers like you are more likely to buy a product from a brand with an excellent reputation in the market, despite being more expensive.

The Dow Jones Industrial Average is the most popular blue-chip company list. 'The Wall Street Journal' editors choose a list of 30 stocks, and for a company to appear in this list, it must be an industry leader. In order for the Dow Jones to come up with a comprehensive list of prestigious blue-chip companies, potential companies are thoroughly scrutinized. Due to blue-chip stocks' inherent stability, the companies making up the Dow Jones index almost never changes.

Blue-Chip Stock Investment

You can invest in blue-chip stock in a number of ways. You can buy stock directly via a direct stock buying plan, a broker, or even a dividend reinvestment plan. You can also buy a blue-chip stock mutual fund, or ETF (Exchange Traded Fund), like the Industrial Average of SPDR Dow Jones that is known to feature a portfolio that reflects the index it is named after. By investing in this kind of stock, you get shares in big companies like McDonald's, Exxon Mobil, Walmart, Microsoft, Coca-Cola, and Disney, among others, for a low expense-ratio and one brokerage commission.

Although you can sell your blue-chip stock, it is always a difficult decision that must be thought over seriously.

Stock Market Capitalization

This simply refers to the market value of the outstanding shares of a company. For example, if Coca-Cola Company has 2 million shares, each at $50, the company's market capitalization would be $100 million. Market capitalization can help you compare and understand the size of two different companies.

Disadvantages of Market Capitalization

Market capitalization has some shortcomings that you should know as someone planning to venture into this market. For one, it cannot be used when looking into the debt of a company. When you buy stock in a company, its true worth is its market capitalization minus its debts, and that is what is known as an enterprise value.

Portfolio Development Using Market Capitalization

When you become a professional investor in this market, like many others, you get to divide your portfolio by the size of the company's market capitalization. This technique can enable you to exploit the stability of larger companies with greater stability and high dividend payouts, and smaller companies with faster historical growth. When you start investing in the stock market, you will come across the following categories of market capitalization: micro, small, mid, large and mega-caps.

Microcap is a company whose market capitalization is below $300 million, small cap $300 million to $2 billion, mid-cap $2 billion to $10 billion, large-cap $10 billion to $50 billion, and mega-cap over $50 billion.

Chapter 3: How The Stock Market Works

In stock market investing, there are two kinds of investors. There are those investors interested in getting dividends and there are those who are interested in buying low and selling high. Therefore, even as you start investing in the stock market, it is important that you determine what kind of investor you are. Are you only interested in getting dividends or are you interested in the fluctuation of stock prices so that you can sell the stock when the price increases.

After a company's IPO, you continue to trade its shares because the company's value changes with time. Depending on your perception's alignment with the stock market, you can either make or lose money. The different traders and investors who buy and sell shares in the market can cause the share price to rise or drop. For instance, if traders get wind of some information that would increase the price of a particular stock, every trader would want to buy such a stock and in the process of buying with the demand being high, this can actually increase the price of the stock.

Due to the demand and supply forces in the stock market, stock prices fluctuate daily. When there is a high demand for shares in the market, prices rise, whereas more supply of shares coupled with low demand leads to dropping prices. Although you can easily understand the demand and supply of shares, making out what drives people to choose select shares and avoid others is very difficult.

Theoretically, the fluctuation of stock prices indicates that a company is considered worthy by investors. The value of a company, which is its market capitalization, (as discussed above) is never equivalent to its stock prices. However, stock prices reflect how investors perceive the company's future growth, and its prevailing market value. It is a company's earnings or profits that determine its value. A firm's earning projection can be used to analyze its future.

When a company performs well and its profits are quite high, their share prices are likely to rise, and if they have poor results, share prices drop. Investors' attitudes, sentiments, and expectations, price or earnings ratio, and the Chaikin oscillator, or the divergence of the moving average convergence also affect stock prices.

Usually it is always advisable to buy stocks when they are low in price. However, practice caution because you don't want to purchase shares of a company whose share price is falling only for it to go bankrupt and you end up losing your investment.

Volume

Volume is the number of shares that change hands within a day. Millions of shares are issued on major stock exchanges like the NASDAQ, or NYSE, meaning that thousands of investors can decide to either buy or sell shares on any given day. Investors usually prefer stock exchanges with high volumes, because they can buy or sell shares easily, because there is always a buyer wanting to buy shares and a seller selling. Furthermore, since particular companies trading in exchanges are mandated to provide volume, it is possible for you to sell a small number of shares even when no one is trading or there is an insufficient volume.

The companies mandated to provide volume in exchanges are known as Market Makers because they act as stock sellers and buyers when no one is trading stock. The reason you should always trade stocks when an exchange has volume is the fact that market makers cannot stop prices from either rising or dropping. Today, most 'market makers' are automated and electronic in nature.

How to Buy Stocks

You can buy stocks through brokerages, DRIPs (dividend reinvestment plans) & DIPs (direct investment plans), a 401k plan, or an IRA. Brokerages can either be full service or discount with the former managing your investment accounts, and providing expert advice. The latter provides cheaper services and gives little attention, making stock investment accessible to everyone. DRIPs and DIPs can enable you to buy shares using small amounts of money.

Stock Price Fluctuation - Causes

Before investing in the stock market, it is important that you conduct research on a specific market and familiarize yourself with it, and find out the merits of putting your money in the stock market. Some of the documents that you need to research are as follows:

The 10K – this is the most essential document that can provide you with the information you need to know about a given firm. Companies are usually required to file a 10K document with the SEC (Securities and Exchange Commission) every year.

The 10Q – this is a smaller version of the 10K document that is filed every quarter.

The Proxy Statement – this document features information about the company's management, board of directors, their pay, and proposals made by shareholders.

Annual Report – you can read reports written by the company CEO, chairman, CFO, and other officers with high ranks to determine their perception of the company. The Berkshire Hathaway's Warren Buffett is considered the best; you can download it free online from the firm's business site.

5 or 10-Year Statistics – most companies usually prepare this document that can provide you with the most relevant information about the company.

The Financial Statements

Before buying a company's stock, you also need to have a look at three of its critical financial statements: the income statement, the cash flow statement, and the balance sheet. These statements go hand in hand, hence you cannot choose to go through one or two and forego the others. Whether you want to invest in bonds or shares, request all three financial statements. They contain the data that can help you make an informed decision before investing in the stock market.

How Stocks Trade

Exchanges can be either physical or virtual, with the former comprising of trading floors and the latter a network of computers. Stock markets are intended to lower investment risks, and facilitate the buying and selling of shares, dubbed securities. In primary stock markets, securities or shares are created, whereas in secondary stock markets you can trade shares that were initially issued without the company in question being involved.

When referring to the stock market, it is the secondary market being discussed; the company whose shares are traded is never involved in this stock market.

The New York Stock Exchange

The NYSE (New York Stock Exchange) is the world's most prestigious exchange. 24 merchants and stockbrokers in New York City signed the Buttonwood Agreement in 1792 to form the 'Big Board,' making the exchange more than 200 years old. As the choice of many large American companies, the NYSE trades shares of companies like Coca-Cola, Wal-Mart, McDonald's, General Electric, and Gillette, among others.

Also dubbed a listed exchange, NYSE is a physical exchange with trading taking place on a trading floor. Brokerage firms with exchange memberships give orders to floor brokers who visit particular spots on the trading floor, called the trading post, where shares are sold and bought. A specialist sits on the trading post and his/her role entails matching sellers and buyers. An auction method is used to determine stock prices with the prevailing price being the highest that a buyer can pay and the least a seller can let go of his/her shares.

The brokerage firm then receives the transaction details, which are sent to the investor. Although the NYSE is a physical exchange, the whole trading process is computerized.

The NASDAQ Exchange

NASDAQ is a popular virtual exchange whose trading occurs through an OTC (over-the-counter) market. Trading occurs through dealer computers and networks. Several large technology companies like Intel, Microsoft, Oracle and Cisco trade over this exchange, making this virtual exchange a major competitor of the NYSE.

In this exchange, brokerages are the market makers that offer bids continually, and request stock prices within a spread and prescribed share percentage. They also maintain stock inventory in order to meet investor's demands, in addition to matching up sellers and buyers.

Other Exchanges

Other exchanges you should know are AMEX (American Stock Exchange), the London Stock Exchange, and the Hong Kong Stock Exchange. OTCBB (over-the-counter bulletin board) trades penny stocks that do not meet regulated stock market requirements; with barely any regulations, stocks in this market are associated with high risks.

Chapter 4: Stock Table or Quote – Interpretation

All financial papers feature stock quotes. Let's go over the main areas you should know.

52W high	52W low	Stock	Ticker	Div	Yield %	P/E	Vol 00s	High	Low	Close	Net chg
$45.39	19.75	ResMed	RMD			52.5	3831	42.00	39.51	41.50	-1.90
11.63	3.55	Revlon A	REV				162	6.09	5.90	6.09	+0.12
77.25	55.13	RioTinto	RTP	2.30	3.2		168	72.75	71.84	72.74	+0.03
31.31	16.63	RitchieBr	RBA			20.9	15	24.49	24.29	24.49	-0.01
8.44	1.75	RiteAid	RAD				31028	4.50	4.20	4.31	+0.21
s38.63	18.81	RobtHalf	RHI			26.5	6517	27.15	26.50	26.50	+0.14
51.25	27.69	Rockwell	ROK	1.02	2.1	14.5	6412	47.99	47.00	47.54	+0.24

Column 1, Column 2, Column 3, Column 4, Column 5, Column 6, Column 7, Column 8, Column 9, Column 10, Column 11, Column 12

(52-Week High & Low): Columns 1 & 2 - These two columns feature the stock's highest and lowest prices traded over the last year (52 weeks). The trading that occurred within the previous day is not featured.

Company Name & Stock Type: Column 3 - Column 3 features the company name and stock type. Common stocks are not followed by letters or special symbols, which stand for different share classes. For instance, 'pf' stands for preferred stock.

Ticker Symbol: Column 4 – Stocks are identified by this distinct alphabetic name. You can use ticker symbols to find a company's stock quotes online. Ticker tapes are used during financial news to indicate the latest stock prices together with the ticker symbol. You can find the ticker of popular companies on Yahoo Finance or Google Finance.

Dividend per Share: Column 5 - This showcases the dividend payments sent by the company every year per share. Blank spaces indicate that the company in question does not pay out dividends to its shareholders by the time the stock table or quote was printed.

Dividend Yield: Column 6 - This is the percentage the dividend returns, which is calculated by dividing the annual dividends per share with the price per stock.

The Ratio of Earnings or Price: Column 7 – The prevailing stock price is divided by the company's earnings per share from the previous 4 quarters to attain this ratio.

Trading Volume: Column 8 - This column indicates the total number of stocks, in hundreds, bought or sold for the day.

Day High and Low: Column 9 & 10 - This showcases the day's stock price range.

Close: Column 11 – This is the stock's last trading price before the market closed for the day.

Net Change: Column 12 - This is the stock's first price the next day after closing the previous day.

Quotes on the Internet –You can access up-to-date stock quotes on the internet, in addition to the latest news, information, research, charting, etc.

In order to succeed in stock market investing, you need to think like a winner and ride with the winners. Avoid penny stocks, select a strategy, and follow it to the end. Adopt a long-term perspective, focus on the future, be open-minded, and always pay your taxes without worrying about them.

Conclusion

When you invest in stocks, you can earn big if your share prices appreciate, and you can receive large dividend payouts which makes for an excellent source of passive income.

As the stock market is unpredictable and no one knows the future, this book cannot really give you any investment advice. However, I will say that as a long term investment strategy, it's best to purchase shares of companies that you think have the highest growth potential going into the long-term, as that's the way all the big stock investors play it. As companies like this are the ones most likely to provide you with the greatest return on your investment after a period of many years.

The ball is now in your hands to invest in this lucrative market. Go forth young investor, with the knowledge you have learned in this book and start investing!